LIFE
Lessons
WITH MAX LUCADO

BOOKS OF COLOSSIANS & PHILEMON

THE DIFFERENCE CHRIST MAKES

MAX LUCADO

Prepared by

THE LIVINGSTONE CORPORATION

Published by
THOMAS NELSON™
Since 1798
www.thomasnelson.com

Material for the "Inspiration" sections taken from the following books:
And the Angels Were Silent. Copyright © 1992, 2004 by Max Lucado. W Publishing Group, a Division of Thomas Nelson, Inc., Nashville, Tennessee.
The Applause of Heaven. Copyright © 1990, 1996, 1999 by Max Lucado. W Publishing Group, a Division of Thomas Nelson, Inc., Nashville, Tennessee.
Come Thirsty. Copyright © 2004 by Max Lucado. W Publishing Group, a Division of Thomas Nelson, Inc., Nashville, Tennessee.
Cure for the Common Life. Copyright © 2005 by Max Lucado. W Publishing Group, a Division of Thomas Nelson, Inc., Nashville, Tennessee.
A Gentle Thunder. Copyright © 1995 by Max Lucado. W Publishing Group, a Division of Thomas Nelson, Inc., Nashville, Tennessee.
God Came Near. Copyright © 2004 by Max Lucado. W Publishing Group, a Division of Thomas Nelson, Inc., Nashville, Tennessee.
The Great House of God. Copyright © 1997 by Max Lucado. W Publishing Group, a Division of Thomas Nelson, Inc., Nashville, Tennessee.
It's Not About Me. Copyright © 2004 by Max Lucado. Integrity Publishers, Brentwood, Tennessee.
A Love Worth Giving. Copyright © 2002 by Max Lucado, W Publishing Group, a Division of Thomas Nelson, Nashville, Tennessee.
Next Door Savior. Copyright © 2003 by Max Lucado. W Publishing Group, a Division of Thomas Nelson, Inc., Nashville, Tennessee.
Six Hours One Friday. Copyright © 2004 by Max Lucado. W Publishing Group, a Division of Thomas Nelson, Inc., Nashville, Tennessee.

Produced with the assistance of the Livingstone Corporation. Project staff include Jake Barton, Joel Bartlett, Andy Culbertson, Mary Horner Collins, Will Reaves, and Rachel Hawkins.
Editor: Len Woods
Cover Art and Interior Design by Kirk Luttrell of the Livingstone Corporation
Interior Composition by Rachel Hawkins of the Livingstone Corporation

ISBN-10: 1-4185-0973-6
ISBN-13: 978-1-4185-0973-6

Printed in the United States of America.
HB 05.31.2019

LIFE
Lessons

WITH MAX LUCADO

CONTENTS

HOW TO STUDY THE BIBLE

This is a peculiar book you are holding. Words crafted in another language. Deeds done in a distant era. Events recorded in a far-off land. Counsel offered to a foreign people. This is a peculiar book.

It's surprising that anyone reads it. It's too old. Some of its writings date back five thousand years. It's too bizarre. The book speaks of incredible floods, fires, earthquakes, and people with supernatural abilities. It's too radical. The Bible calls for undying devotion to a carpenter who called himself God's Son.

Logic says this book shouldn't survive. Too old, too bizarre, too radical.

The Bible has been banned, burned, scoffed, and ridiculed. Scholars have mocked it as foolish. Kings have branded it as illegal. A thousand times over, the grave has been dug and the dirge has begun, but somehow the Bible never stays in the grave. Not only has it survived; it has thrived. It is the single most popular book in all of history. It has been the best-selling book in the world for years!

There is no way on earth to explain it. Which perhaps is the only explanation. The answer? The Bible's durability is not found on earth; it is found in heaven. For the millions who have tested its claims and claimed its promises, there is but one answer: the Bible is God's book and God's voice.

As you read it, you would be wise to give some thought to two questions. What is the purpose of the Bible? and How do I study the Bible? Time spent reflecting on these two issues will greatly enhance your Bible study.

What is the purpose of the Bible?

Let the Bible itself answer that question.

Since you were a child you have known the Holy Scriptures which are able to make you wise. And that wisdom leads to salvation through faith in Christ Jesus. (2 Tim. 3:15 NCV)

The purpose of the Bible? Salvation. God's highest passion is to get his children home. His book, the Bible, describes his plan of salvation. The purpose of the Bible is to proclaim God's plan and passion to save his children.

That is the reason this book has endured through the centuries. It dares to tackle the toughest questions about life: Where do I go after I die? Is there a God? What do I do with my fears? The Bible offers answers to these crucial questions. It is the treasure map that leads us to God's highest treasure, eternal life.

But how do we use the Bible? Countless copies of Scripture sit unread on bookshelves and nightstands simply because people don't know how to read it. What can we do to make the Bible real in our lives?

The clearest answer is found in the words of Jesus. He promised:

Ask, and God will give to you. Search, and you will find. Knock, and the door will open for you. (Matt. 7:7 NCV)

The first step in understanding the Bible is asking God to help us. We should read prayerfully. If anyone understands God's Word, it is because of God and not the reader.

But the Helper will teach you everything and will cause you to remember all that I told you. The Helper is the Holy Spirit whom the Father will send in my name. (John 14:26 NCV)

Before reading the Bible, pray. Invite God to speak to you. Don't go to Scripture looking for your idea; go searching for his.

Not only should we read the Bible prayerfully; we should read it carefully. *Search and you will find* is the pledge. The Bible is not a newspaper to be skimmed but rather a mine to be quarried.

Search for it like silver, and hunt for it like hidden treasure. Then you will understand respect for the LORD, and you will find that you know God. (Prov. 2:4–5 NCV)

Any worthy find requires effort. The Bible is no exception. To understand the Bible you don't have to be brilliant, but you must be willing to roll up your sleeves and search.

Be a worker who is not ashamed and who uses the true teaching in the right way. (2 Tim. 2:15 NCV)

Here's a practical point. Study the Bible a bit at a time. Hunger is not satisfied by eating twenty-one meals in one sitting once a week. The body needs a steady diet to remain strong. So does the soul. When God sent food to his people in the wilderness, he didn't provide loaves already made. Instead, he sent them manna in the shape of *"thin flakes like frost . . . on the desert ground"* (Ex. 16:14 NCV).

God gave manna in limited portions. God sends spiritual food the same way. He opens the heavens with just enough nutrients for today's hunger. He provides *"a command here, a command there. A rule here, a rule there. A little lesson here, a little lesson there"* (Isa. 28:10 NCV).

Don't be discouraged if your reading reaps a small harvest. Some days a lesser portion is all that is needed. What is important is to search every day for that day's message. A steady diet of God's Word over a lifetime builds a healthy soul and mind.

A little girl returned from her first day at school. Her mom asked, "Did you learn anything?"

"Apparently not enough," the girl responded, "I have to go back tomorrow and the next day and the next . . ."

Such is the case with learning. And such is the case with Bible study. Understanding comes little by little over a lifetime.

There is a third step in understanding the Bible. After the asking and seeking comes the knocking. After you ask and search, then knock.

Knock, and the door will open for you. (Matt. 7:7 NCV)

To knock is to stand at God's door. To make yourself available. To climb the steps, cross the porch, stand at the doorway, and volunteer. Knocking goes beyond the realm of thinking and into the realm of acting.

To knock is to ask, What can I do? How can I obey? Where can I go?

It's one thing to know what to do. It's another to do it. But for those who do it, those who choose to obey, a special reward awaits them.

The truly happy are those who carefully study God's perfect law that makes people free, and they continue to study it. They do not forget what they heard, but they obey what God's teaching says. Those who do this will be made happy. (James 1:25 NCV)

What a promise. Happiness comes to those who do what they read! It's the same with medicine. If you only read the label but ignore the pills, it won't help. It's the same with food. If you only read the recipe but never cook, you won't be fed. And it's the same with the Bible. If you only read the words but never obey, you'll never know the joy God has promised.

Ask. Search. Knock. Simple, isn't it? Why don't you give it a try? If you do, you'll see why you are holding the most remarkable book in history.

INTRODUCTION TO THE BOOK OF COLOSSIANS

The renowned British author C. S. Lewis once noted that most Christians need reminding more than they need instruction. How insightful. How true.

We are a forgetful people. Sadly, when we lose sight of God's amazing promises to us, his marvelous provisions for us, it is our all-too-common tendency to become proud.

We forget how desperate we were. We forget how merciful God has been. If we are not careful, we may begin to see salvation not as the toss of the life preserver to the drowning but as a journey in a rowboat: God's grace handling one oar and our noble efforts handling the other. It's not that Jesus isn't necessary; it's just that Jesus needs our assistance. We may even start imagining that God is lucky to have us on his team.

Slowly, subtly, we begin to embrace the doctrine of *salvation by Jesus plus*. Jesus plus good deeds. Jesus plus the right doctrine. Jesus plus the right Bible translation.

Or in the case of the church in Colossae, Jesus plus the right religious feast, New Moon Festival, and Sabbath day. To the Christians in Colossae, the right rituals were every bit as important as the right Savior.

Paul would have none of this. He denounced the Jesus-plus philosophy as heretical. If we are saved, he insisted, it is only because God mercifully plucked us out of the deep and not because we scrambled into his boat, grabbed an oar, and started paddling.

Let the book of Colossians remind you of the great truth that Jesus is our all-in-all. He is all our souls need, and all our hearts desire. We become different and we make a difference by ordering our lives around the incomparable Christ.

LESSON ONE

FAITH, HOPE, AND LOVE

MAX
LUCADO

REFLECTION

Letter writing is quickly becoming a relic of a bygone era. With cell phones, text messaging and e-mail, very few people sit down anymore with paper and pen, with the intent of composing a thoughtful correspondence. What are your own letter-writing habits?

SITUATION

Colossians is Paul's letter to a church that was being bombarded by an eclectic mix of heretical teachings. His message: Christ is preeminent. He is Creator and Lord—the all-sufficient Savior of the world. In our union with him—by grace and through faith—the Christian finds all he or she will ever need.

OBSERVATION

Read Colossians 1:1–8 from the NCV or the NKJV.

NCV

[1]From Paul, an apostle of Christ Jesus. I am an apostle because that is what God wanted. Also from Timothy, our brother.

[2]To the holy and faithful brothers and sisters in Christ that live in Colossae:

Grace and peace to you from God our Father.

[3]In our prayers for you we always thank God, the Father of our Lord Jesus Christ, [4]because we have heard about the faith you have in Christ Jesus and the love you have for all of God's people. [5]You have this faith and love because of your hope, and what you hope for is kept safe for you in heaven. You learned about this hope when you heard the message about the truth, the Good News [6]that was told to you. Everywhere in the world that Good News is bringing blessings and is growing. This has happened with you, too, since you heard the Good News and understood the truth about the grace of God. [7]You learned about God's grace from Epaphras, whom we love. He works together with us and is a faithful servant of Christ for us. [8]He also told us about the love you have from the Holy Spirit.

NKJV

[1]Paul, an apostle of Jesus Christ by the will of God, and Timothy our brother,

[2]To the saints and faithful brethren in Christ who are in Colosse:

Grace to you and peace from God our Father and the Lord Jesus Christ.

[3]We give thanks to the God and Father of our Lord Jesus Christ, praying always for you, [4]since we heard of your faith in Christ Jesus and of your love for all the saints; [5]because of the hope which is laid up for you in heaven, of which you heard before in the word of the truth of the gospel, [6]which has come to you, as it has also in all the world, and is bringing forth fruit, as it is also among you since the day you heard and knew the grace of God in truth; [7]as you also learned from Epaphras, our dear fellow servant, who is a faithful minister of Christ on your behalf, [8]who also declared to us your love in the Spirit.

EXPLORATION

1. What do we learn about the Colossians from this brief introductory paragraph?

2. Why was Paul thankful for the Colossians?

3. What does the Bible mean when it speaks of "hope"?

4. What is the connection between faith, hope, and love?

5. What do you remember most about the day when you "understood the truth about the grace of God" (v. 6 NCV)?

INSPIRATION

Jesus said, "I am the bread that gives life. I am the light of the world. I am the resurrection and the life . . . I am the door. I am the way, the truth, and the life. I will come back and take you with me."

Jesus proclaiming—ever offering but never forcing:

Standing over the crippled man: *"Do you want to be well?"* (John 5:6 NCV).

Eye to eye with the blind man, now healed: *"Do you believe in the Son of Man?"* (John 9:35).

Near the tomb of Lazarus, probing the heart of Martha: *"Everyone who lives and believes in me will never die. Martha, do you believe this?"* (John 11:26).

Testing Pilate's motive: *"Is that your own question, or did others tell you about me?"* (John 18:34).

The first time John hears Jesus speak, Jesus asks a question, *"What are you looking for?"* (John 1:38). Among Jesus' last words is yet another: *"Do you love me?"* (21:17).

This is the Jesus John remembers. The honest questions. The thundering claims. The gentle touch. Never going where not invited, but once invited never stopping until he's finished, until a choice has been made.

God will whisper. He will shout. He will touch and tug. He will take away our burdens; he'll even take away our blessings. If there are a thousand steps between us and him, he will take all but one. But he will leave the final one for us. The choice is ours.

Please understand. His goal is not to make you happy. His goal is to make you his. His goal is not to get you what you want; it is to get you what you need . . . Earthly discomfort is a glad swap for heavenly peace. Jesus said, *"In this world you will have trouble, but be brave! I have defeated the world"* (John 16:33). (From *A Gentle Thunder* by Max Lucado)

REACTION

6. The Colossians heard the claims of Christ from Epaphras. Whom did God use to share the good news with you?

7. Paul referred to his readers as "holy" (v. 2 NCV), a word that means being set apart or dedicated solely for God's use. What are the practical implications of this?

8. What about your life would prompt your pastor or small-group leader or mentor to feel thankful?

9. How is the gospel bearing fruit and growing in your life?

10. How can we tell if we are demonstrating "love in the Spirit" (v. 8 NKJV)?

11. What does it mean to be a "saint"?

LIFE LESSONS

Amazing things happen when we put our faith in Christ. We are born again (John 3). We become God's children (John 1). Our sins are forgiven (Eph. 1). We receive eternal life (1 John 5). God's Spirit takes up residence in our lives (Rom. 8). Not only do we enjoy all these blessings, but we also are infused with hope. Biblical hope is not a vague wish about the future; it is a sure and certain expectation. With that hope, we also receive a new capacity to love others. Faith, hope, and love. These are the defining marks of one who has experienced new life in Christ!

DEVOTION

Father in heaven, thank you for opening my eyes—my heart—to the truth of the gospel. Deepen my faith. Strengthen my hope. Increase my love. Cause the gospel to bear much fruit in and through my life. In the great name of Christ, I pray.

For more Bible passages on faith, hope, and love, see Romans 5:1–5; 1 Corinthians 13:13; Galatians 5:5–6; 1 Thessalonians 1:3; 5:8; and 1 Peter 1:21–22.

To complete the books of Colossians and Philemon during this twelve-part study, read Colossians 1:1–8.

JOURNALING

How does a deep and abiding hope in Christ lead to a life filled with love?

LESSON TWO

PRAYING
WITH POWER

MAX
LUCADO

REFLECTION

Right now, all over the world, Christians are praying. In trucks. In elevators. In barracks. Stuck in traffic. Waiting outside ICUs. Talking to God. Listening to him. Thanking him for amazing blessings. Asking him for "impossible" miracles. Who are the people who faithfully pray for you? Who are the ones you want praying for you?

SITUATION

The church at Colossae was founded by Epaphras, a ministry associate of the apostle Paul. Though Paul had never visited the church, he prayed faithfully for them—for their growth and maturity, especially in the face of false teaching.

OBSERVATION

Read Colossians 1:9–14 from the NCV or the NKJV.

NCV

9Because of this, since the day we heard about you, we have continued praying for you, asking God that you will know fully what he wants. We pray that you will also have great wisdom and understanding in spiritual things 10so that you will live the kind of life that honors and pleases the Lord in every way. You will produce fruit in every good work and grow in the knowledge of God. 11God will strengthen you with his own great power so that you will not give up when troubles come, but you will be patient. 12And you will joyfully give thanks to the Father who has made you able to have a share in all that he has prepared for his people in the kingdom of light. 13God has freed us from the power of darkness, and he brought us into the kingdom of his dear Son. 14The Son paid for our sins, and in him we have forgiveness.

NKJV

9For this reason we also, since the day we heard it, do not cease to pray for you, and to ask that you may be filled with the knowledge of His will in all wisdom and spiritual understanding; 10that you may walk worthy of the Lord, fully pleasing Him, being fruitful in every good work and increasing in the knowledge of God; 11strengthened with all might, according to His glorious power, for all patience and longsuffering with joy; 12giving thanks to the Father who has qualified us to be partakers of the inheritance of the saints in the light. 13He has delivered us from the power of darkness and conveyed us into the kingdom of the Son of His love, 14in whom we have redemption through His blood, the forgiveness of sins.

EXPLORATION

1. How would you describe your prayer habits for other people?

2. What are the specific things Paul requests, and which of these virtues or abilities do you need most?

3. Note the content of Paul's prayer for the Colossians. How do his petitions for them compare to the kinds of prayers you offer for others?

4. What truths about God and his gifts to us does Paul mention as the foundation for his requests?

5. Paul's prayers were very Christ focused, very God centered. How does a deep knowledge of God enhance a Christian's prayer life?

INSPIRATION

The key to knowing God's heart is having a relationship with him. A *personal* relationship. God will speak to you differently than he will speak to others. Just because God spoke to Moses through a burning bush, that doesn't mean we should all sit next to a bush waiting for God to speak. God used a fish to convict Jonah. Does that mean we should have worship services at Sea World? No. God reveals his heart personally to each person.

For that reason, your walk with God is essential. His heart is not seen in an occasional chat or weekly visit . . .

If you were to take a name at random out of the phone book and ask me, "Max, how does Chester Whomever feel about adultery?" I couldn't answer. I don't know Chester Whomever. But if you were to ask me, "Max, how does Denalyn Lucado feel about adultery?" I wouldn't even have to call her. I know. She's my wife. We have walked together long enough that I know what she thinks.

The same is true with God. Walk with him long enough and you come to know his heart. When you spend time with him in his study, you see his passion. Welcome him to enter the gateway of your soul and you'll perceive his will.
(From *The Great House of God* by Max Lucado)

REACTION

6. Would you characterize your prayer life as a continual conversation with God or an occasional chat? Why?

7. Why do you think the prayers offered in so many groups tend to be "safe" (i.e., for Aunt Martha's neighbor who has cancer) rather than personal (i.e., for my struggle with envy)? How can we avoid this?

8. What advice would you give a new Christian who is trying to establish a healthy prayer life?

9. What percentage of your prayers is focused on your own needs and desires versus the needs of others?

10. What do you think about keeping a prayer list or prayer journal?

11. What are two changes you want to make in your own prayer life?

LIFE LESSONS

Someone has quipped, "I don't understand much about the great mystery of prayer. I just know this: When I pray, God does amazing things, and when I don't pray, not much happens." Though it's hard to fathom, it's true: the Lord has ordained for our prayers to play a key role in the building of his kingdom! So what are the basic New Testament guidelines for effective praying? Pray unselfishly and with a pure heart (James 4:3). Pray relentlessly (1 Thess. 5:17). Pray believing that God will work (Mark 11:24). Pray according to God's will (John 15:7). Most of all, pray with a heart that is surrendered to God's ultimate purposes (Luke 22:42).

DEVOTION

God, fill me with the knowledge of your will. Grant me spiritual wisdom and insight so that I might live the kind of life that pleases you. Make me fruitful and help me to know you more and more as I live in your infinite strength.

For more Bible passages on prayer, see Psalm 66:18; Mark 1:35; Philippians 4:6–7; James 1:6; 5:16; and 1 John 3:22.

To complete the books of Colossians and Philemon during this twelve-part study, read Colossians 1:9–14.

JOURNALING

Put Paul's prayer from Colossians 1 in your own words, and personalize it to your life and those in your family.

LESSON THREE

THE
SUPREMACY
OF CHRIST

MAX
LUCADO

REFLECTION

History is filled with interesting and remarkable characters. Imagine throwing a dinner party and getting to invite any eight people, living or dead, great or obscure. Who would be on your guest list and why?

Mother, daughter Mary & Joseph FDR

SITUATION

When he realized the Colossian Christians were being subjected to all kinds of weird and false religious notions, Paul wrote them to remind them of this basic message: Jesus Christ is God in the flesh. He created and sustains the universe. As the Savior of the world, he is all our souls will ever need.

OBSERVATION

Read Colossians 1:15–23 from the NCV or the NKJV.

NCV

15No one can see God, but Jesus Christ is exactly like him. He ranks higher than everything that has been made. 16Through his power all things were made—things in heaven and on earth, things seen and unseen, all powers, authorities, lords, and rulers. All things were made through Christ and for Christ. 17He was there before anything was made, and all things continue because of him. 18He is the head of the body, which is the church. Everything comes from him. He is the first one who was raised from the dead. So in all things Jesus has first place. 19God was pleased for all of himself to live in Christ. 20And through Christ, God has brought all things back to himself again—things on earth and things in heaven. God made peace through the blood of Christ's death on the cross.

21At one time you were separated from God. You were his enemies in your minds, and the evil things you did were against God. 22But now God has made you his friends again. He did this through Christ's death in the body so that he might bring you into God's presence as people who are holy, with no wrong, and with nothing of which God can judge you guilty. 23This will happen if you continue strong and sure in your faith. You must not be moved away from the hope brought to you by the Good News that you heard. That same Good News has been told to everyone in the world, and I, Paul, help in preaching that Good News.

NKJV

15He is the image of the invisible God, the firstborn over all creation. 16For by Him all things were created that are in heaven and that are on earth, visible and invisible, whether thrones or dominions or principalities or powers. All things were created through Him and for Him. 17And He is before all things, and in Him all things consist. 18And He is the head of the body, the church, who is the beginning, the firstborn from the dead, that in all things He may have the preeminence.

19For it pleased the Father that in Him all the fullness should dwell, 20and by Him to reconcile all things to Himself, by Him, whether things on earth or things in heaven, having made peace through the blood of His cross.

21And you, who once were alienated and enemies in your mind by wicked works, yet now He has reconciled 22in the body of His flesh through death, to present you holy, and blameless, and above reproach in His sight— 23if indeed you continue in the faith, grounded and steadfast, and are not moved away from the hope of the gospel which you heard, which was preached to every creature under heaven, of which I, Paul, became a minister.

EXPLORATION

1. What is significant about the words and phrases Paul uses to describe Christ's nature in this passage?

2. How does this description compare with the way many in our culture view Christ?

Jesus, Prophett

3. What does it mean that *"in all things Jesus has first place"* (v. 18 NCV)?

4. In describing Christ's saving work, Paul refers to his readers, before their conversion, as being God's "enemies" (v. 21). Why does he use this term?

Reflection

5. How do you explain Christ (who he is and what he did) to friends who are not Christians?

INSPIRATION

Make no mistake, Jesus saw himself as God. He leaves us with two options. Accept him as God, or reject him as a megalomaniac. There is no third alternative.

Oh, but we try to create one. Suppose I did the same? Suppose you came across me standing on the side of the road. I can go north or south. You ask me which way I'm going. My reply? "I'm going sorth."

Thinking you didn't hear me correctly, you ask me to repeat the answer.

"I'm going sorth. I can't choose between north and south, so I'm going both. I'm going sorth."

"You can't do that," you reply. "You have to choose."

"OK," I concede, "I'll head nouth."

"Nouth is not an option!" you insist. "It's either north or south. One way or the other. To the right or to the left. When it comes to this road, you gotta pick."

When it comes to Christ, you've got to do the same. Call him crazy, or crown him as king. Dismiss him as a fraud, or declare him to be God. Walk away from him, or bow down before him, but don't play games with him. Don't call him a great man. Don't list him among decent folk. Don't clump him with Moses, Elijah, Buddha, Joseph Smith, Muhammad, or Confucius. He didn't leave that option. He is either God or godless. Heaven sent or hell born. All hope or all hype. But nothing in between. (From *Next Door Savior* by Max Lucado)

REACTION

6. Do you agree with such logic—that Christ must be regarded as either Lord of all, or as a lunatic/liar? *Lord*

7. How would it affect your life today if you consciously remembered that "all things were made through Christ and *for Christ*" (v. 16 NCV, emphasis added)?

8. Paul challenges his readers to continue in the faith, to not be "moved away from the hope brought to you" (v. 23 NCV). What things have the potential to move you away from Christ today?

9. How can a wrong understanding of Christ's nature or ignorance of his work affect us in profound ways?

10. What are the most prominent people, things, or desires in your life that compete with Christ's lordship?"

11. What three practical changes can you make in your thinking, schedule, etc., to reflect the supremacy of Christ in your life today?

LIFE LESSONS

In our noisy and flashy world, it is the "new and improved" that gets all the attention. We notice big and loud things. We focus on bizarre, shocking things. And we like upgrades. We are ever looking to trade in and trade up. The more trendy, the more off-beat, the more appealing to our image-conscious culture. The result is that the "old, old story" of the gospel is increasingly seen as trite and outdated. Why follow Jesus, a figure from antiquity, when we can follow the latest New Age guru? Because, as Paul reminds us, Jesus is the beginning and end of everything. All knowledge and power and beauty and mystery and meaning are found in him. He is the only one who can satisfy the deepest hungers of our hearts. The restless search of the human race ends at the cross of Christ.

DEVOTION

Lord Jesus, thank you for making and saving and sustaining me. I enthrone you now as the king of my life. Give me eyes to see you. Give me ears to hear you. Give me courage to show and share you with the watching world.

For more Bible passages on the preeminence of Christ, see John 1:1–18; Ephesians 1:22–23; Hebrews 1:1–3; and Revelation 5:1–14.

To complete the books of Colossians and Philemon during this twelve-part study, read Colossians 1:15–23.

JOURNALING

Describe what Christ means to you.

L E S S O N   F O U R

SERVING CHRIST

MAX
LUCADO

REFLECTION

There's a pretty consistent phenomenon at work in the average church. It goes like this: "*Twenty* percent of the members and active attenders do *eighty* percent of the serving and giving." Ponder that for a few moments. How do we account for such an imbalance?

SITUATION

While imprisoned for preaching the gospel, the apostle Paul wrote this short letter of encouragement to some Christians he had never met. In it, he urged them to resist false teachings about Christ and to persevere in the faith, through trials and discouragements, relying always on the infinite power of Christ.

OBSERVATION

Read Colossians 1:24–29 from the NCV or the NKJV.

NCV

24I am happy in my sufferings for you. There are things that Christ must still suffer through his body, the church. I am accepting, in my body, my part of these things that must be suffered. 25I became a servant of the church because God gave me a special work to do that helps you, and that work is to tell fully the message of God. 26This message is the secret that was hidden from everyone since the beginning of time, but now it is made known to God's holy people. 27God decided to let his people know this rich and glorious secret which he has for all people. This secret is Christ himself, who is in you. He is our only hope for glory. 28So we continue to preach Christ to each person, using all wisdom to warn and to teach everyone, in order to bring each one into God's presence as a mature person in Christ. 29To do this, I work and struggle, using Christ's great strength that works so powerfully in me.

NKJV

²⁴I now rejoice in my sufferings for you, and fill up in my flesh what is lacking in the afflictions of Christ, for the sake of His body, which is the church, ²⁵of which I became a minister according to the stewardship from God which was given to me for you, to fulfill the word of God, ²⁶the mystery which has been hidden from ages and from generations, but now has been revealed to His saints. ²⁷To them God willed to make known what are the riches of the glory of this mystery among the Gentiles: which is Christ in you, the hope of glory. ²⁸Him we preach, warning every man and teaching every man in all wisdom, that we may present every man perfect in Christ Jesus. ²⁹To this end I also labor, striving according to His working which works in me mightily.

EXPLORATION

1. How can a person honestly rejoice in the face of sufferings?

2. What makes the "mystery" of verses 26–27 (NKJV) so amazing? (Hint: Go back and reread 1:15–19.)

3. What does it mean to be, as Paul described himself, a servant of the church?

4. How did Paul sum up his mission, and in what ways should this be our mission too?

5. The prophets, the apostles, the early church—all devoted to God, all committed to serving him, all constantly in trouble. Why? Why do Christians face so many trials?

INSPIRATION

The brevity of life grants power to abide, not an excuse to bail. Fleeting days don't justify fleeing problems. Fleeting days strengthen us to endure problems. Will your problems pass? No guarantee they will. Will your pain cease? Perhaps. Perhaps not. But heaven gives this promise: *"our light affliction, which is but for a moment, is working for us a far more exceeding and eternal weight of glory"* (2 Cor. 4:17 NKJV).

The words "weight of glory" conjure up images of the ancient pan scale. Remember the blindfolded lady of justice? She holds a pan scale—two pans, one on either side of the needle. The weight of a purchase would be determined by placing weights on one side and the purchase on the other.

God does the same with your struggles. On one side he stacks all your burdens. Famines. Firings. Parents who forgot you. Bosses who ignored you. Bad breaks, bad health, bad days. Stack them up, and watch one side of the pan scale plummet.

Now witness God's response. Does he remove them? Eliminate the burdents? No, rather than take them, he offsets them. He places an eternal weight of glory on the other side. Endless joy. Measureless peace. An eternity of him. Watch what happens as he sets eternity on your scale.

Everything changes! The burdens lift. The heavy becomes light when weighed against eternity. If life is "just for a moment," can't we endure any challenge for a moment?

We can be sick for *just a moment.*

We can be lonely for *just a moment.*

We can be persecuted for *just a moment.*

We can struggle for *just a moment.*

Can't we?

Can't we wait for our peace? It's not about us anyway. And it's certainly not about now. (From *It's Not About Me* by Max Lucado)

REACTION

6. Read 2 Corinthians 4:16–18. How *does* such an eternal perspective put our sufferings in a new and different light?

7. How can one Christian's sufferings be in the interest of, or be beneficial to other believers?

8. What are the trials, big and small, that you are currently facing in your life?

9. As you think about tomorrow or the week ahead, what practical difference does it make that Christ, the hope of glory, is "*in* you" (v. 27)?

10. As an apostle, Paul served by teaching and preaching. How has God gifted you to serve others?

11. Christian service involves us laboring (literally, toiling to the point of exhaustion) as we rely on the Lord's infinite strength. What's the hardest you've labored for your church?

LIFE LESSONS

If Christ were merely *with* us, that would be fantastic. But even more amazing is the New Testament declaration that he is *in* us. Think of it—the Prince of Peace, the Good Shepherd, the great I AM—living in our hearts. The implications are positively staggering! The possibilities are infinite! What did Paul do with such mind-boggling truth? Simple. He served. He poured out his life for others. And why not? After all, the Christ who filled him (and the same Jesus who lives in us) described himself as one who came not to be served, but to serve. The more we realize the truth of Christ "in us," the more we are willing to use our gifts and energy to bless others, no matter what hardships come.

DEVOTION

Lord Jesus, thank you for making your home in me. What an amazing mystery, and what a hopeful truth! I can do all things through Christ. Help me to labor in service to others with all the strength you give.

For more Bible passages on serving, see Mark 10:43–45; John 13:14; 2 Corinthians 4:11; 12:7–10; Galatians 6:2, 10; Philippians 2:5–8; and 1 Peter 4:10–11.

To complete the books of Colossians and Philemon during this twelve-part study, read Colossians 1:24–29.

JOURNALING

God's desire is for us to become mature servants. Describe the areas in which you need to grow most.

LESSON FIVE

WALKING
WITH CHRIST

MAX
LUCADO

REFLECTION

"Why don't you guys practice what you preach?" Surely this charge—the allegation of hypocrisy—is the biggest knock against Christians and the Christian faith. And it is a curious dilemma. How do you explain the common tendency among so many believers to be "spiritually schizophrenic"—acting one way at certain times and in totally different ways in other settings?

SITUATION

Paul, the missionary with a pastor's heart, writes to Colossian believers whom he has never met to encourage them to center their lives on the Lord Jesus Christ. In a world of competing philosophies and conflicting belief systems, Christ is the source of ultimate wisdom and meaning.

OBSERVATION

Read Colossians 2:1–10 from the NCV or the NKJV.

NCV

¹I want you to know how hard I work for you, those in Laodicea, and others who have never seen me. ²I want them to be strengthened and joined together with love so that they may be rich in their understanding. This leads to their knowing fully God's secret, that is, Christ himself. ³In him all the treasures of wisdom and knowledge are safely kept.

⁴I say this so that no one can fool you by arguments that seem good, but are false. ⁵Though I am absent from you in my body, my heart is with you, and I am happy to see your good lives and your strong faith in Christ.

⁶As you received Christ Jesus the Lord, so continue to live in him. ⁷Keep your roots deep in him and have your lives built on him. Be strong in the faith, just as you were taught, and always be thankful.

⁸Be sure that no one leads you away with false and empty teaching that is only human, which comes from the ruling spirits of this world, and not from Christ. ⁹All of God lives in Christ fully (even when Christ was on earth), ¹⁰and you have a full and true life in Christ, who is ruler over all rulers and powers.

NKJV

¹For I want you to know what a great conflict I have for you and those in Laodicea, and for as many as have not seen my face in the flesh, ²that their hearts may be encouraged, being knit together in love, and attaining to all riches of the full assurance of understanding, to the knowledge of the mystery of God, both of the Father and of Christ, ³in whom are hidden all the treasures of wisdom and knowledge.

⁴Now this I say lest anyone should deceive you with persuasive words. ⁵For though I am absent in the flesh, yet I am with you in spirit, rejoicing to see your good order and the steadfastness of your faith in Christ.

⁶As you therefore have received Christ Jesus the Lord, so walk in Him, ⁷rooted and built up in Him and established in the faith, as you have been taught, abounding in it with thanksgiving.

⁸Beware lest anyone cheat you through philosophy and empty deceit, according to the tradition of men, according to the basic principles of the world, and not according to Christ. ⁹For in Him dwells all the fullness of the Godhead bodily; ¹⁰and you are complete in Him, who is the head of all principality and power.

EXPLORATION

1. How is it possible to have a deep spiritual concern for people one has never met?

2. How does a person learn to distinguish between "true truth" and "arguments that seem good, but are false" (v. 4 NCV)?

3. Paul urges his readers toward a more stable, solid faith. What are some practical indications that one is maturing spiritually?

4. What is Paul's counsel to the person who is hungry for true wisdom and seeking spiritual enlightenment?

5. Notice all the references to being "in Christ" or "in him." Why is this idea so significant?

INSPIRATION

God can be your dwelling place.

God *wants* to be your dwelling place. He has no interest in being a weekend getaway or a Sunday bungalow or a summer cottage. Don't consider using God as a vacation cabin or an eventual retirement home. He wants you under his roof now and always. He wants to be your mailing address, your point of reference; he wants to be your home. Listen to the promise of his Son, *"If my people love me, they will obey my teaching. My Father will love them and we will come to them and make our home with them"* (John 14:23 NCV).

For many this is a new thought. We think of God as a deity to discuss, not a place to dwell. We think of God as a mysterious miracle worker, not a house to live in. We think of God as a creator to call on, not a home to reside in. But our Father wants to be much more. He wants to be the one in whom *"we live and move and have our being"* (Acts 17:28 NIV).

When Jehovah led the children of Israel through the wilderness, he didn't just appear once a day and then abandon them. The pillar of fire was present all night; the cloud was present all day. Our God never leaves us. *"I will be with you always,"* he promised (Matt. 28:20 NCV). Our faith takes a quantum leap when we understand the perpetual presence of the Father. Our Jehovah is the fire of our night and the cloud of our day. He never leaves us.

Heaven knows no difference between Sunday morning and Wednesday afternoon. God longs to speak as clearly in the workplace as he does in the sanctuary. He longs to be worshiped when we sit at the dinner table and not just when we come to his communion table. You may go days without thinking of him, but there's never a moment when he's not thinking of you. (From *The Great House of God* by Max Lucado)

REACTION

6. How does living in Christ or walking with him moment by moment differ from the way many Christians view faith?

7. Hollywood has put the life of Christ on film numerous times. Which—if any—of these movies have prompted you to seek a deeper faith in him?

8. How would you explain verse 6 to a brand-new Christian?

9. The Colossians were blessed to have a strong spiritual mentor like Paul. Who are the older, wiser saints who exhort you in the faith?

10. What does it mean to be "complete in Him" (v. 10 NKJV) or to "have a full and true life in Christ" (NCV)?

11. Paul uses the metaphor of being rooted in Christ. How can you develop stronger, deeper spiritual roots this week?

LIFE LESSONS

Like a CD player that keeps playing the same track over and over and over, Paul keeps coming back to the same theme: Christ is enough, because Christ is ultimate. There is no higher truth. There is no other source of fulfillment. We can search the world over looking for wisdom; we can spend our lives hunting for meaning and inner peace. But only in Christ do we find the answers that our souls crave. *"In him all the treasures of wisdom and knowledge are safely kept"* (v. 3 NCV). The search for satisfaction ends at the feet of Jesus. And there the great journey, the lifelong adventure of faith, begins as I begin my walk with you.

DEVOTION

Lord Jesus, I received you by faith, therefore I must continue to live in you by faith. In a world filled with false ideas, grant me the grace and wisdom to learn to discern. Continually remind me that in you "are all the treasures of wisdom and knowledge."

For more Bible passages on the Christian walk, see John 15:1–11; Romans 6:4; 2 Corinthians 5:7; Galatians 5:16–25; Ephesians 4:1; and 1 John 1:6–7.

To complete the books of Colossians and Philemon during this twelve-part study, read Colossians 2:1–10.

JOURNALING

In your spiritual walk just now, what are your biggest struggles?

LESSON SIX

"PHOOLISH"
PHILOSOPHIES

MAX
LUCADO

REFLECTION

Survivalist sects in Montana. Polygamous groups in Utah. Hollywood stars trumpeting Scientology. Atheistic scholars advocating naturalism. The fact is, our culture has almost as many worldviews as we've got people! What anti-Christian philosophies or extrabiblical religious beliefs are popular in your locale?

SITUATION

The apostle Paul, under house arrest in Rome, wrote to challenge the Christians in Colossae to cut through all the bogus and obsolete spiritual clutter of their culture and to make Jesus Christ the center of their faith.

OBSERVATION

Read Colossians 2:11–23 from the NCV or the NKJV.

NCV

[11]Also in Christ you had a different kind of circumcision, a circumcision not done by hands. It was through Christ's circumcision, that is, his death, that you were made free from the power of your sinful self. [12]When you were baptized, you were buried with Christ, and you were raised up with him through your faith in God's power that was shown when he raised Christ from the dead. [13]When you were spiritually dead because of your sins and because you were not free from the power of your sinful self, God made you alive with Christ, and he forgave all our sins. [14]He canceled the debt, which listed all the rules we failed to follow. He took away that record with its rules and nailed it to the cross. [15]God stripped the spiritual rulers and powers of their authority. With the cross, he won the victory and showed the world that they were powerless.

¹⁶So do not let anyone make rules for you about eating and drinking or about a religious feast, a New Moon Festival, or a Sabbath day. ¹⁷These things were like a shadow of what was to come. But what is true and real has come and is found in Christ. ¹⁸Do not let anyone disqualify you by making you humiliate yourself and worship angels. Such people enter into visions, which fill them with foolish pride because of their human way of thinking. ¹⁹They do not hold tightly to Christ, the head. It is from him that all the parts of the body are cared for and held together. So it grows in the way God wants it to grow.

²⁰Since you died with Christ and were made free from the ruling spirits of the world, why do you act as if you still belong to this world by following rules like these: ²¹"Don't eat this," "Don't taste that," "Don't even touch that thing"? ²²These rules refer to earthly things that are gone as soon as they are used. They are only man-made commands and teachings. ²³They seem to be wise, but they are only part of a man-made religion. They make people pretend not to be proud and make them punish their bodies, but they do not really control the evil desires of the sinful self.

NKJV

¹¹In Him you were also circumcised with the circumcision made without hands, by putting off the body of the sins of the flesh, by the circumcision of Christ, ¹²buried with Him in baptism, in which you also were raised with Him through faith in the working of God, who raised Him from the dead. ¹³And you, being dead in your trespasses and the uncircumcision of your flesh, He has made alive together with Him, having forgiven you all trespasses, ¹⁴having wiped out the handwriting of requirements that was against us, which was contrary to us. And He has taken it out of the way, having nailed it to the cross. ¹⁵Having disarmed principalities and powers, He made a public spectacle of them, triumphing over them in it.

¹⁶So let no one judge you in food or in drink, or regarding a festival or a new moon or sabbaths, ¹⁷which are a shadow of things to come, but the substance is of Christ. ¹⁸Let no one cheat you of your reward, taking delight in false humility and worship of angels, intruding into those things which he has not seen, vainly puffed up by his fleshly mind, ¹⁹and not holding fast to the Head, from whom all the body, nourished and knit together by joints and ligaments, grows with the increase that is from God.

²⁰Therefore, if you died with Christ from the basic principles of the world, why, as though living in the world, do you subject yourselves to regulations— ²¹"Do not touch, do not taste, do not handle," ²²which all concern things which perish with the using— according to the commandments and doctrines of men? ²³These things indeed have an appearance of wisdom in self-imposed religion, false humility, and neglect of the body, but are of no value against the indulgence of the flesh.

EXPLORATION

1. How would you explain the difference between the Jewish rite of circumcision and the spiritual circumcision Paul mentions in verses 11–12?

2. Why did Paul in his letters come back again and again to the cross of Christ (compare Colossians 2:13–15 with 1 Corinthians 1:23 and 2:8)?

3. Paul talks about some of the rigid religious rules advocated in ancient Colossae. What legalistic, man-made restrictions are common in your church or spiritual circle?

4. Why do religious people and institutions get so uncomfortable with spiritual freedom and try so hard to control others?

5. How can we distinguish between healthy, God-honoring spiritual guidelines, and man-made religious rules?

INSPIRATION

If you've always thought of Jesus as a pale-faced, milquetoast Tiny Tim, then read Matthew 23 and see the other side: an angry father denouncing the pimps who have prostituted his children.

Six times he calls them hypocrites. Five times he calls them blind. Seven times he denounces them and once he prophesies their ruin. Not what you would call a public relations presentation.

But in the midst of the roaring river of words there is a safe island of instruction. Somewhere between bursts of fire Jesus holsters his pistol, turns to the wide-eyed disciples, and describes the essence of simple faith. Four verses: a reading as brief as it is practical. Call it Christ's solution to complicated Christianity.

"You must not be called 'Teacher,' because you have only one Teacher, and you are all brothers and sisters together. And don't call any person on earth 'Father,' because you have one Father, who is in heaven. And you should not be called 'Master,' because you have only one Master, the Christ. Whoever is your servant is the greatest among you. Whoever makes himself great will be made humble. Whoever makes himself humble will be made great" (Matt. 23:8–12 NCV).

How do you simplify your faith? How do you get rid of the clutter? How do you discover a joy worth waking up to? Simple. Get rid of the middleman.

Discover truth for yourself. *"You have only one Teacher, and you are all brothers and sisters together"* (v. 8).

Develop trust for yourself. *"Don't call any person on earth 'Father,' because you have one Father, who is in heaven"* (v. 9).

Discern his will for yourself. *"You have only one Master, the Christ"* (v. 10).

There are some who position themselves between you and God. There are some who suggest the only way to get to God is through them. There is the great teacher who has the final word on Bible teaching. There is the father who must bless your acts. There is the spiritual master who will tell you what God wants you to do. Jesus' message for complicated religion is to remove these middlemen.

He's not saying that you don't need teachers, elders, or counselors. He is saying, however, that we are all brothers and sisters and have equal access to the Father. Simplify your faith by seeking God for yourself. No confusing ceremonies necessary. No mysterious rituals required. No elaborate channels of command or levels of access.

You have a Bible? You can study. You have a heart? You can pray. You have a mind? You can think. (From *And the Angels Were Silent* by Max Lucado)

REACTION

6. When it comes to matters of faith, how much do you rely on God's indwelling Spirit to be your Counselor and Guide, and how much do you just do what other Christians tell you to do?

7. How does a church steer clear of the dangerous ways of legalism?

8. How can an individual believer avoid being swept away by the subtle winds of spiritual error?

9. The Colossians were influenced by asceticism—the shunning of anything that might result in physical pleasure or comfort. What's so "spiritual" about such a lifestyle?

10. Angel worship was an ancient practice. Why do angels appeal to us today?

11. Why are external rules incapable of bringing about internal reformation?

LIFE LESSONS

As followers of Jesus, we must remain on high alert. Both Scripture and history show how easy it is for well-meaning, but naïve Christians to become sidetracked by the exotic claims of religious cults and the pride-enticing allure of modern philosophies. Only one person is worthy of our minds' attention and our hearts' affection—Jesus Christ. "What is true and real has come and is found in" him (v. 17 NCV). If you are laboring in vain to keep a long list of man-made religious rules, if you are confused by the competing claims of fast-talking spiritual gurus, remember that Christ came to set us free. Push aside the spiritual static of all the other voices. Open the gospels and listen again to the still, small voice of Christ.

DEVOTION

Father in heaven, thank you for revealing yourself in Christ. Not only did he die for my sins, but he rose again to show me how I need to live and where I need to go. Help me grow in my faith so that I can distinguish between the genuine leading of your Spirit and the counterfeit promptings of the evil one.

For more Bible passages on suspect spirituality, see 1 Timothy 4:1–7; 2 Timothy 3:1–9; Titus 1:10–16; 2 Peter 2:1–22; 2 John 7–11; and Jude 3–16.

To complete the books of Colossians and Philemon during this twelve-part study, read Colossians 2:11–23.

JOURNALING

Do you engage in any activities that other Christians frown upon? How do you know if they are being legalistic toward you or if you are guilty of license (i.e., being too lax in your faith)?

LESSON SEVEN

LIVING
DIFFERENTLY

MAX
LUCADO

REFLECTION

Inner fulfillment. A new and different life. This is what we all hunger for. What else can explain the way we change churches, switch spouses, and swap jobs? What other reason can account for the way we consume goods and services, the boom in plastic surgery, the growth of certain cults? What are the biggest and most satisfying changes you've undergone?

SITUATION

In contrast to the intriguing, but impotent religious ideas making the rounds in Colossae, Paul wanted the Christians there to remember that a deep and personal relationship with God through Christ effectively transforms every aspect of a believer's life.

OBSERVATION

Read Colossians 3:1–17 from the NCV or the NKJV.

NCV

1Since you were raised from the dead with Christ, aim at what is in heaven, where Christ is sitting at the right hand of God. 2Think only about the things in heaven, not the things on earth. 3Your old sinful self has died, and your new life is kept with Christ in God. 4Christ is our life, and when he comes again, you will share in his glory.

5So put all evil things out of your life: sexual sinning, doing evil, letting evil thoughts control you, wanting things that are evil, and greed. This is really serving a false god. 6These things make God angry. 7In your past, evil life you also did these things.

8But now also put these things out of your life: anger, bad temper, doing or saying things to hurt others, and using evil words when you talk. 9Do not lie to each other. You have left your old sinful life and the things you did before. 10You have begun to live the new life, in which you are being made new and are becoming like the One who made you. This new life brings you the true knowledge of God. 11In the new life there is no difference between Greeks and Jews, those who are circumcised and those who are not circumcised, or people who are foreigners, or Scythians. There is no difference between slaves and free people. But Christ is in all believers, and Christ is all that is important.

12God has chosen you and made you his holy people. He loves you. So always do these things: Show mercy to others, be kind, humble, gentle, and patient. 13Get along with each other, and forgive each other. If someone does wrong to you, forgive that person because the Lord forgave you. 14Do all these things; but most important, love each other. Love is what holds you all together in perfect unity. 15Let the peace that Christ gives control your thinking, because you were all called together in one body to have peace. Always be thankful. 16Let the teaching of Christ live in you richly. Use all wisdom to teach and instruct each other by singing psalms, hymns, and spiritual songs with thankfulness in your hearts to God. 17Everything you do or say should be done to obey Jesus your Lord. And in all you do, give thanks to God the Father through Jesus.

NKJV

1If then you were raised with Christ, seek those things which are above, where Christ is, sitting at the right hand of God. 2Set your mind on things above, not on things on the earth. 3For you died, and your life is hidden with Christ in God. 4When Christ who is our life appears, then you also will appear with Him in glory.

5Therefore put to death your members which are on the earth: fornication, uncleanness, passion, evil desire, and covetousness, which is idolatry. 6Because of these things the wrath of God is coming upon the sons of disobedience, 7in which you yourselves once walked when you lived in them.

8But now you yourselves are to put off all these: anger, wrath, malice, blasphemy, filthy language out of your mouth. 9Do not lie to one another, since you have put off the old man with his deeds, 10and have put on the new man who is renewed in knowledge according to the image of Him who created him, 11where there is neither Greek nor Jew, circumcised nor uncircumcised, barbarian, Scythian, slave nor free, but Christ is all and in all.

12Therefore, as the elect of God, holy and beloved, put on tender mercies, kindness, humility, meekness, longsuffering; 13bearing with one another, and forgiving one another, if anyone has a complaint against another; even as Christ forgave you, so you also must do. 14But above all these things put on love, which is the bond of perfection. 15And let the peace of God rule in your hearts, to which also you were called in one body; and be thankful. 16Let the word of Christ dwell in you richly in all wisdom, teaching and admonishing one another in psalms and hymns and spiritual songs, singing with grace in your hearts to the Lord. 17And whatever you do in word or deed, do all in the name of the Lord Jesus, giving thanks to God the Father through Him.

EXPLORATION

1. How does a person seek those things or set his or her mind on things above?

2. What does Paul mean when he says our "life is hidden with Christ in God" (v. 3 NKJV) and "Christ is our life" (v. 4 NCV)?

3. Paul contrasts two ways of life: an old way and a new way, with Christ making the difference. Has Christ made such a radical difference in your own life?

4. What aspects of new life in Christ do you need to "wear" more consistently?

5. It almost sounds as if Paul is saying, "You want to change? Okay . . . Stop sinning." Why is this so easy to say and so difficult to do?

INSPIRATION

Accept this invitation of Jesus: *"Abide in My love"* (John 15:9 NASB).

When you abide somewhere, you live there. You grow familiar with the surroundings. You don't pull in the driveway and ask, "Where is the garage?" You don't consult the blueprint to find the kitchen. To abide is to be at home.

To abide in Christ's love is to make his love your home. Not a roadside park or hotel room you occasionally visit, but your preferred dwelling. You rest in him. Eat in him. When thunder claps, you step beneath his roof. His walls secure you from the winds. His fireplace warms you from the winters of life. As John urged, *"We take up permanent residence in a life of love"* (1 John 4:16 MSG). You abandon the old house of false love and move into his home of real love.

Adapting to this new home takes time. First few nights in a new home you can wake up and walk into a wall. I did. Not in a new home, but in a motel. Climbed out of bed to get a glass of water, turned left, and flattened my nose. The dimensions to the room were different.

The dimensions of God's love are different too. You've lived a life in a house of imperfect love. You think God is going to cut you as the coach did, or abandon you as your father did, or judge you as false religion did, or curse you as your friend did. He won't, but it takes time to be convinced.

For that reason, abide in him. Hang on to Christ the same way a branch clutches the vine. According to Jesus, the branch models his definition of *abiding*. *"As the branch cannot bear fruit of itself unless it abides in the vine, so neither can you unless you abide in Me"* (John 15:4 NASB). (From *Come Thirsty* by Max Lucado)

REACTION

6. Do you feel "at home in Christ"? Why or why not?

7. Of the wrong attitudes and actions that Paul mentions, which habits do you most struggle with?

8. Remember, verses 12–17 are written to a whole church. Does the description here fit your church or small group?

9. How forgiving are you?

10. What relationship in your life is currently giving you the most trouble? Why do you think?

11. How can we cultivate a more thankful attitude in life?

LIFE LESSONS

Call it what you will—the gospel message or the Christian faith—the fact is, the kind of spirituality advocated by Christ was never meant to be a neat religious theory. As someone has said, Jesus didn't come to give us a lot of new information; rather he came that we might undergo transformation. He does this by first forgiving us and wiping the slate clean. Then he does something odd but powerful. He moves us into himself and moves himself into us. In other words, we are united with him fundamentally and eternally. He becomes both our life and our Lord. And he will never rest until we are changed, until our character is just like his.

DEVOTION

O Father! What a wonderful promise. The good work you have begun in me will continue until its completion. Thank you for new life. I open my heart to you now and invite you to do your transforming work. I want to make my home in you, and I want you to be at home in me.

For more Bible passages on holy living, see Psalm 15; Ephesians 5:1–19; Philippians 4:1–9; 1 Thessalonians 4:1–12; and 1 Peter 4:1–11.

To complete the books of Colossians and Philemon during this twelve-part study, read Colossians 3:1–17.

JOURNALING

Meditating on Colossians 3:12–17, comment on your own obedience to each of these commands.

LESSON EIGHT

HOME,
SWEET HOME

MAX
LUCADO

REFLECTION

A number of recent surveys indicate that the divorce rate among Christians is not substantially lower than the divorce rate among the general population. Other studies suggest that many of the problems that plague irreligious families are also common in Christian families. How do we account for these facts? Why does the gospel seem to be so irrelevant in so many Christian homes?

SITUATION

The apostle Paul's best counsel to a church struggling both to be different and to make a difference in a spiritually confused culture? Let the truth of Christ shine in your marriages and families!

OBSERVATION

Read Colossians 3:18–21 from the NCV or the NKJV.

NCV

¹⁸Wives, yield to the authority of your husbands, because this is the right thing to do in the Lord.

¹⁹Husbands, love your wives and be gentle with them.

²⁰Children, obey your parents in all things, because this pleases the Lord.

²¹Fathers, do not nag your children. If you are too hard to please, they may want to stop trying.

NKJV

¹⁸Wives, submit to your own husbands, as is fitting in the Lord.

¹⁹Husbands, love your wives and do not be bitter toward them.

²⁰Children, obey your parents in all things, for this is well pleasing to the Lord.

²¹Fathers, do not provoke your children, lest they become discouraged.

EXPLORATION

1. Why is there such heated controversy regarding the biblical command that wives should "submit" (NKJV) or "yield to the authority of [their] husbands" (NCV)?

2. How might most of this furor subside if men humbly and consistently lived out verse 19?

3. What were the rules your parents made you obey as a child?

4. What are some ways dads nag their children or provoke them to discouragement?

5. What marriages or families do you most admire and why?

INSPIRATION

Every time we ate at home, my mom gave my brother and me the same instructions: "Put a little bit of everything on your plate."

We never had to be told to clean the plate. Eating volume was not a challenge. Variety was. Don't get me wrong, Mom was a good cook. But boiled okra? Asparagus? More like "croak-ra" and "gasp-aragus." Were they really intended for human consumption?

According to Mom, they were, and—according to Mom—they had to be eaten. "Eat some of everything." That was the rule in our house.

But that was not the rule at the cafeteria. On special occasions we made the forty-five minute drive to the greatest culinary innovation since the gas stove: the cafeteria line. Ah, what a fine moment indeed to take a tray and gaze down the midway at the endless options. A veritable cornucopia of fine cuisine. Down the row you walk, intoxicated by the selection and liberated by the freedom. Yes to the fried fish; no to the fried tomatoes. Yes to the pecan pie; no, no, a thousand times no to the "croak-ra" and "gasp-aragus." Cafeteria lines are great.

Wouldn't it be nice if love were like a cafeteria line? What if you could look at a person with whom you live and select what you want and pass on what you don't? What if parents could do this with kids? "I'll take a plate of good grades and cute smiles, and I'm passing on the teenage identity crisis and tuition bills."

What if kids could do the same with parents? "Please give me a helping of allowances and free lodging but no rules or curfews, thank you."

And spouse with spouse? "H'm, how about a bowl of good health and good moods. But job transfers, in-laws, and laundry are not on my diet."

Wouldn't it be great if love were like a cafeteria line? It would be easier. It would be neater. It would be painless and peaceful. But you know what? It wouldn't be love. Love doesn't accept just a few things. Love is willing to accept all things.

God's view of love is like my mom's view of food. When we love someone, we take the entire package. No picking and choosing. No large helpings of the good and passing on the bad. Love is a package deal. (From *A Love Worth Giving* by Max Lucado)

REACTION

6. How well is your family showing love to each other right now?

7. Why does submitting or deferring to someone else not imply that one is inferior to that person? (Hint: see 1 Corinthians 11:3.)

8. In what way does Ephesians 5:25 expand and elaborate on this command that husbands love their wives?

9. How did your parents discipline you?

10. What are the most discouraging things that you see parents do to their kids?

11. What three actions could you take today that would immediately make your home more peaceful, loving, and God honoring?

LIFE LESSONS

Someone has well said, "If our faith doesn't work at home, our faith doesn't work." Nowhere is it more crucial that we put our beliefs into practice and on display. So ask yourself a few hard questions: Is your relationship with Jesus noticeable by the way you talk to your family members? By the way in which you listen? How about in the way you resolve conflicts? Is your family happy to see you come home (or secretly more glad to see you leave)? Do you serve your spouse and encourage your kids? Is there an atmosphere of respect and gentleness in your home? When is the last time you made a sacrifice for someone else, putting his or her needs before your own desires?

DEVOTION

Father, we could use some home improvements in our family. Remind me that I can't change anyone but myself, and I can't even do that without your help. Strengthen me today to do my part—to fulfill my family role in a way that pleases you and promotes peace.

For more Bible passages on the home and family, see Genesis 2:23–24; Deuteronomy 5:16; Psalm 127:3; Proverbs 22:6, 15; Ephesians 5:22–6:4; 1 Timothy 3:4, 11, 15; and 1 Peter 3:1–7.

To complete the books of Colossians and Philemon during this twelve-part study, read Colossians 3:18–21.

JOURNALING

What are your best memories from your growing-up years with your family?

WHAT ABOUT WORK?

MAX LUCADO

REFLECTION

Just by reading bumper stickers ("Work fascinates me . . . I can sit and watch it for hours!" or "I owe, I owe—it's off to work I go"), one can tell that most people view their jobs as a necessary evil. What about you? In fifty words or less, summarize your feelings about your occupation or vocation.

SITUATION

Since 50 percent or more of the residents of the Roman empire were slaves, Paul addresses how Christ makes a difference in master-slave relationships. Here we find some great principles for how Christian employers and employees should live and interact.

OBSERVATION

Read Colossians 3:22—4:1 from the NCV or the NKJV.

NCV

²²*Slaves, obey your masters in all things. Do not obey just when they are watching you, to gain their favor, but serve them honestly, because you respect the Lord. ²³In all the work you are doing, work the best you can. Work as if you were doing it for the Lord, not for people. ²⁴Remember that you will receive your reward from the Lord, which he promised to his people. You are serving the Lord Christ. ²⁵But remember that anyone who does wrong will be punished for that wrong, and the Lord treats everyone the same.*

¹*Masters, give what is good and fair to your slaves. Remember that you have a Master in heaven.*

NKJV

²²*Bondservants, obey in all things your masters according to the flesh, not with eye-service, as men-pleasers, but in sincerity of heart, fearing God. ²³And whatever you do, do it heartily, as to the Lord and not to men, ²⁴knowing that from the Lord you will receive the reward of the inheritance; for you serve the Lord Christ. ²⁵But he who does wrong will be repaid for what he has done, and there is no partiality.*

¹*Masters, give your bondservants what is just and fair, knowing that you also have a Master in heaven.*

EXPLORATION

1. Why do you think Paul and the other apostles didn't completely condemn slavery?

2. How did biblical teachings like this and Galatians 3:28 pave the way for the eventual abolition of slavery?

3. What do you make of the fact that work existed before the Fall and before sin ever entered the world (Gen. 2:15)?

4. What's the best job you've ever had?

5. Who is the best boss or employer you've ever had and why?

INSPIRATION

Heaven's calendar has seven Sundays a week. God sanctifies each day. He conducts holy business at all hours and in all places. He uncommons the common by turning kitchen sinks into shrines, cafés into convents, and nine-to-five workdays into spiritual adventures.

Workdays? Yes, workdays. He ordained your work as something good. Before he gave Adam a wife or a child, even before he gave Adam britches, God gave Adam a job. *"Then the Lord God took the man and put him into the garden of Eden to cultivate it and keep it"* (Gen. 2:15 NASB). Innocence, not indolence, characterized the first family.

God views work worthy of its own engraved commandment: *"You shall work six days, but on the seventh day you shall rest"* (Exod. 34:21 NASB). We like the second half of that verse. But emphasis on the day of rest might cause us to miss the command of work: "You *shall* work six days." Whether you work at home or in the marketplace, your work matters to God.

And your work matters to society. We need you! Cities need plumbers. Nations need soldiers. Stoplights break. Bones break. We need people to repair the first and set the second. Someone has to raise kids, raise cane, and manage the kids who raise Cain.

Whether you log on or lace up for the day, you imitate God. Jehovah himself worked for the first six days of creation. Jesus said, *"My Father never stops working, and so I keep working, too"* (John 5:17 NCV). Your career consumes half of your lifetime. Shouldn't it broadcast God? Don't those forty to sixty hours a week belong to him as well? (From *Cure for the Common Life* by Max Lucado)

REACTION

6. Do you have a hard time viewing work as a spiritual activity? Why or why not?

7. What is the proper motivation for work?

8. What factors make you unmotivated at work and tempt you to do less than your best?

9. If you were an employer, what practices or policies would you implement to stimulate your workers to do their best?

10. Who is the hardest-working person you know? What makes him or her such a good worker?

II. List three practical things you can do today to help develop a better attitude regarding your job, your supervisor, or your coworkers?

LIFE LESSONS

Unless you were born with a silver spoon in your mouth and a pile of gold bullion in the bank, you will have to work, perhaps even *labor* and *toil* in this life. It isn't a pleasant thought, but it's true nonetheless, that every occupation in a fallen world—working alongside fallen coworkers and for fallen bosses—involves frustration and calls for tough choices. We can work grimly or gladly, make mediocrity our goal or commit ourselves to excellence. Paul tells us that Christians should never do just enough to get by. We should do our work "heartily" (v. 23 NKJV)—with a good attitude and an all-out effort. After all, it is the Lord Christ whom we serve, and to whom we will one day give an account (2 Cor. 5:10).

DEVOTION

Lord, thank you for the reminder that my occupation matters to you. This week, in my attitude, my work ethic, and habits, may I make you smile. And, as a bonus, may I have a positive impact on those in my workplace. Those are wages enough.

For more Bible passages on work, see Genesis 3:19; Deuteronomy 24:15; Proverbs 10:4; 12:11; 13:4; 22:29; Ephesians 6:5–9; 1 Timothy 6:1; Titus 2:9; and 1 Peter 2:18.

To complete the books of Colossians and Philemon during this twelve-part study, read Colossians 3:22–4:1.

JOURNALING

How can someone know when it's time to seek different employment?

A MOUTH
THAT MAKES
A DIFFERENCE

MAX
LUCADO

REFLECTION

We call it by many names. Evangelism. Witnessing. Soul winning. Giving a testimony. What images, positive or negative, come to mind when you hear someone refer to sharing the gospel?

SITUATION

The Colossians lived in a culture permeated with the competing claims of spurious spiritual teachers. Paul's challenge to believers? Open your mouths and speak boldly but gently the only truth that can set men free.

OBSERVATION

Read Colossians 4:2—6 from the NCV or the NKJV.

NCV

²Continue praying, keeping alert, and always thanking God. ³Also pray for us that God will give us an opportunity to tell people his message. Pray that we can preach the secret that God has made known about Christ. This is why I am in prison. ⁴Pray that I can speak in a way that will make it clear, as I should.

⁵Be wise in the way you act with people who are not believers, making the most of every opportunity. ⁶When you talk, you should always be kind and pleasant so you will be able to answer everyone in the way you should.

NKJV

²Continue earnestly in prayer, being vigilant in it with thanksgiving; ³meanwhile praying also for us, that God would open to us a door for the word, to speak the mystery of Christ, for which I am also in chains, ⁴that I may make it manifest, as I ought to speak.

⁵Walk in wisdom toward those who are outside, redeeming the time. ⁶Let your speech always be with grace, seasoned with salt, that you may know how you ought to answer each one.

EXPLORATION

1. Someone has suggested that it's important to talk to God about people, before we talk to people about God. Why?

2. How can a Christian tell when God has opened a door or presented an opportunity for the gospel?

3. What exactly is the clear and simple gospel?

4. How proactively do you look for opportunities to turn conversations toward spiritual issues?

5. Whatever does Paul mean when he says that our conversations with unbelievers should be "seasoned with salt" (v. 6 NKJV)?

INSPIRATION

Think about your first encounter with the Christ. Robe yourself in that moment. Resurrect the relief. Recall the purity. Summon forth the passion. Can you remember?

I can. 1965. A red-headed ten-year-old with a tornado of freckles sits in a Bible class on a Wednesday night. What I remember of the class are scenes—school desks with initials carved in them. A blackboard. A dozen or so kids, some listening, some not. A teacher wearing a suit coat too tight to button around his robust belly.

He is talking about Jesus. He is explaining the cross. I know I had heard it before, but that night I heard it for sure. "You can't save yourself; you need a savior." I can't explain why it connected that night as opposed to another, but it did. He simply articulated what I was beginning to understand—I was lost—and he explained what I needed—a redeemer. From that night on, my heart belonged to Jesus.

Many would argue that a ten-year-old is too young for such a decision. And they may be right. All I know is that I never made a more earnest decision in my life. I didn't know much about God, but what I knew was enough. I knew I wanted to go to heaven. And I knew I couldn't do it alone.

No one had to tell me to be happy. No one had to tell me to tell others. They couldn't keep me quiet. I told all my friends at school. I put a bumper sticker on my bicycle. And though I'd never read 2 Corinthians 4:13, I knew what it meant. "I believed; therefore I have spoken" (NIV). Pardon truly received is pardon powerfully proclaimed.

There is a direct correlation between the accuracy of our memory and the effectiveness of our mission. If we are not teaching people how to be saved, it is perhaps because we have forgotten the tragedy of being lost! If we're not teaching the message of forgiveness, it may be because we don't remember what it was like to be guilty. And if we're not preaching the cross, it could be that we've subconsciously decided that—God forbid—somehow we don't need it. (From *Six Hours One Friday* by Max Lucado)

REACTION

6. What have been your experiences with trying to communicate your faith in Christ? What is your current practice?

7. How consistently do you pray that God would open doors for the gospel message to be shared?

8. What are some signs that God is working in a person's heart and wooing him or her to himself?

9. What exactly needs to be "clear" about the way we present the gospel?

10. What are some wise and unwise ways we can act around those who do not (yet) share our faith?

11. How equipped or prepared do you feel when it comes to articulating what you believe?

LIFE LESSONS

It's important to remember that we can use our tongues for ill or for good. We can gossip and criticize and withhold truth, or we can impact others positively by speaking to them about the life-changing love of Christ. If we want to use our mouths to make an eternal difference (and deep down, every Christian does), we must begin with preparation and prayer. Make sure first that you know how to give a reason for the spiritual hope that is in you (1 Pet. 3:15). Consider attending an evangelism training workshop or working with a fellow Christian with many years of experience of sharing his or her faith. Second, make it your daily practice to pray for opportunities to clearly tell others the good news of forgiveness and new life in Christ.

DEVOTION

Father, life is so short. Remind me daily that I have been given a great treasure and an urgent task—telling others about your grace and love. Make me wise in the way I act around unbelievers. May I be courageous, kind, and clear.

For more Bible passages on making the most of witnessing opportunities, see Mark 5:18–19; John 9:4; Acts 1:8; 21:37–22:1; 1 Corinthians 2:1–5; and Ephesians 5:15–16; 6:19.

To complete the books of Colossians and Philemon during this twelve-part study, read Colossians 4:2–6.

JOURNALING

List the people in your life who do not yet know Christ but who show signs of being interested in the gospel. What unique approach might you need to take with each one in talking about spiritual things?

LESSON ELEVEN

COMPANIONS ON THE JOURNEY

MAX
LUCADO

REFLECTION

The Bible uses a variety of metaphors to describe the church: a body (1 Cor. 12), a living building (Eph. 2:19–22), a temple (2 Cor. 6:16), a spiritual family (John 1:12; 1 John 3:1), a bride (2 Cor. 11:2), and a flock (Acts 20:29). If you were to come up with a symbol or metaphor to describe your local church, what would it be?

SITUATION

Paul concludes his letter to the Colossian church with some final greetings from a variety of colleagues and mutual friends, reminding us that the Christian faith should bring believers together as a single body. God means for his children to live and grow and serve *together*.

OBSERVATION

Read Colossians 4:7–18 from the NCV or the NKJV.

NCV

⁷*Tychicus is my dear brother in Christ and a faithful minister and servant with me in the Lord. He will tell you all the things that are happening to me.* ⁸*This is why I am sending him: so you may know how we are and he may encourage you.* ⁹*I send him with Onesimus, a faithful and dear brother in Christ, and one of your group. They will tell you all that has happened here.*

¹⁰*Aristarchus, a prisoner with me, and Mark, the cousin of Barnabas, greet you. (I have already told you what to do about Mark. If he comes, welcome him.)* ¹¹*Jesus, who is called Justus, also greets you. These are the only Jewish believers who work with me for the kingdom of God, and they have been a comfort to me.*

¹²*Epaphras, a servant of Jesus Christ, from your group, also greets you. He always prays for you that you will grow to be spiritually mature and have everything God wants for you.* ¹³*I know he has worked hard for you and the people in Laodicea and in Hierapolis.* ¹⁴*Demas and our dear friend Luke, the doctor, greet you.*

¹⁵*Greet the brothers in Laodicea. And greet Nympha and the church that meets in her house.* ¹⁶*After this letter is read to you, be sure it is also read to the church in Laodicea. And you read the letter that I wrote to Laodicea.* ¹⁷*Tell Archippus, "Be sure to finish the work the Lord gave you."*

18I, Paul, greet you and write this with my own hand. Remember me in prison. Grace be with you.

NKJV

7Tychicus, a beloved brother, faithful minister, and fellow servant in the Lord, will tell you all the news about me. 8I am sending him to you for this very purpose, that he may know your circumstances and comfort your hearts, 9with Onesimus, a faithful and beloved brother, who is one of you. They will make known to you all things which are happening here.

10Aristarchus my fellow prisoner greets you, with Mark the cousin of Barnabas (about whom you received instructions: if he comes to you, welcome him), 11and Jesus who is called Justus. These are my only fellow workers for the kingdom of God who are of the circumcision; they have proved to be a comfort to me.

12Epaphras, who is one of you, a bondservant of Christ, greets you, always laboring fervently for you in prayers, that you may stand perfect and complete in all the will of God. 13For I bear him witness that he has a great zeal for you, and those who are in Laodicea, and those in Hierapolis. 14Luke the beloved physician and Demas greet you. 15Greet the brethren who are in Laodicea, and Nymphas and the church that is in his house.

16Now when this epistle is read among you, see that it is read also in the church of the Laodiceans, and that you likewise read the epistle from Laodicea. 17And say to Archippus, "Take heed to the ministry which you have received in the Lord, that you may fulfill it."

18This salutation by my own hand—Paul. Remember my chains. Grace be with you. Amen.

EXPLORATION

1. Who are your dearest brothers and sisters in the faith? What makes them important in your life?

2. How would other Christians describe you in a letter to a third party?

3. Why are warm greetings and words of affirmation so important among believers?

4. Why did Paul feel the need to mention that Aristarchus, Mark, and Jesus Justus were Jewish believers?

5. What's the last letter or e-mail you wrote in which your goal was to offer spiritual encouragement?

INSPIRATION

The Bible has its share of . . . saints . . . spurred by a gut-level conviction that they had been called by no one less than God himself. As a result, their work wasn't affected by moods, cloudy days, or rocky trails. Their performance graph didn't rise and fall with roller-coaster irregularity. They weren't addicted to accolades or applause nor deterred by grumpy bosses or empty wallets. Rather than strive to be spectacular, they aspired to be accountable and dependable. And since their loyalty was not determined by their comfort, they were just as faithful in dark prisons as they were in spotlighted pulpits.

Reliable servants. They're the binding of the Bible. Their acts are rarely recited and their names are seldom mentioned. Yet were it not for their loyal devotion to God, many great events never would have occurred . . .

Epaphroditus would be on this list . . . To describe this fellow with the five-syllable name Paul used more succinct words like *brother, fellow worker, fellow soldier,* and *messenger.* You don't earn eulogies like these from appearing at an occasional youth rally or showing up at church picnics. These are compliments earned over years and tears . . . Epaphroditus. The only thing longer than his name was his staying power . . .

Re-liable. *Liable* means responsible. *Re* means over and over again.

I'm wondering if this book has found its way into the hands of some contemporary saints of reliability. If such is the case . . .

Thank you.

Thank you senior saints for a generation of prayer and forest clearing.

Thank you teachers for the countless Sunday school lessons, prepared and delivered with tenderness.

Thank you missionaries for your bravery in sharing the timeless truth in a foreign tongue.

Thank you preachers. You thought we weren't listening, but we were. And your stubborn sowing of God's seed is bearing fruit you may never see this side of the great harvest.

Thanks to all of you who practice on Monday what you hear on Sunday. You spent selfless hours with orphans, at typewriters, in board meetings, on knees, in hospital wards, away from families, and on assembly lines. It is upon the back of your fidelity that the gospel rides. (From *God Came Near* by Max Lucado)

REACTION

6. Who are the specific Christians who, humanly speaking, are responsible for your spiritual life and growth?

7. How can you show thanks to your spiritual leaders and mentors?

8. How are modern-day small groups similar to ancient house churches?

9. Epaphras wrestled in prayer. What are your prayer habits—specifically your habits of praying for other believers?

10. Who needs your encouragement in a fashion similar to the exhortation Paul gave Archippus?

11. Contrast Acts 15:37–40 and Colossians 4:10 with Colossians 4:14 and 2 Timothy 4:10. How do the opposite life trajectories of Mark and Demas sober you?

LIFE LESSONS

At the end of this Christ-centered, theology-drenched letter, Paul concludes with an endearing snapshot of community. Aristarchus, Mark, Jesus Justus, Epaphras, Luke, Demas, Nympha, Archippus . . . ordinary folks serving an extraordinary God in a myriad of ways. The passage is permeated with affection and punctuated with purpose. All alone, these individuals would not have much of an impact. But ministering together they helped turn the first-century world "upside down" (Acts 17:6 NKJV). This is God's design for the Christian life— uniquely gifted people banding together to accomplish his kingdom plan. Resist the modern trends toward individualism and personal autonomy. Link up with other believers to grow and serve.

DEVOTION

Father, thank you for the brief but profound reminder here that in calling us to yourself, you have also called us to one another. Increase my hunger for and commitment to my community of spiritual brothers and sisters.

For more Bible passages on spiritual community, see John 13:34–35; 17; Acts 2:42–47; Romans 12:3–16; 1 Corinthians 12; Galatians 6:1–10; and Ephesians 4:1–16.

To complete the books of Colossians and Philemon during this twelve-part study, read Colossians 4:7–18.

JOURNALING

How is your spiritual community better because of your devotion to it, and how is your life better because of your spiritual community's investment in you?

INTRODUCTION TO THE BOOK OF PHILEMON

Philemon had every reason to be angry. His slave, Onesimus, had stolen from him and run away. Somehow the thief made his way to the metropolis of Rome, where he *just happened* to meet the apostle Paul, who *just happened* to be an old friend of Philemon.

Transformed by the message of Christ, Onesimus, at Paul's request, is now returning to Philemon. Under normal circumstances, Philemon has every right to exact revenge. But these are not normal circumstances. Onesimus fled as a slave; he returns as a believer and a spiritual brother. Paul doesn't ask Philemon to free Onesimus from slavery, but to free him from harsh vengeance. He urges Philemon to offer grace rather than demand justice.

Does this short letter have any application for your life? It does if there is an Onesimus in your world. It does if someone has betrayed you or offended you or turned away from you. Getting even would be the common desire. Demanding justice would be a natural response, which is precisely the problem. Christians aren't called to live naturally, but supernaturally.

As you consider how to respond to someone who has wronged you, consider Paul's exhortation to Philemon. Behind that, ponder the example of Christ. As his followers, our calling is to live by the higher law of God's kingdom, a law which sets all men, slave or nonslave, free.

That is the difference Christ makes.

THE
MIRACLE OF
FORGIVENESS

MAX
LUCADO

REFLECTION

Think back over your childhood, especially your adolescent years. What were one or two of your most regrettable choices or hurtful actions? More importantly, how did those you hurt treat you after the fact?

SITUATION

Onesimus was a slave from Colossae who stole from his master, Philemon, and fled to Rome, where he met Paul, who introduced him to Christ. The apostle sent Onesimus back to Philemon with this letter that encourages mercy, forgiveness, and Christian love.

OBSERVATION

Read Philemon 1:8–21 from the NCV or the NKJV.

NCV

⁸*So, in Christ, I could be bold and order you to do what is right.* ⁹*But because I love you, I am pleading with you instead. I, Paul, an old man now and also a prisoner for Christ Jesus,* ¹⁰*am pleading with you for my child Onesimus, who became my child while I was in prison.* ¹¹*In the past he was useless to you, but now he has become useful for both you and me.*

¹²*I am sending him back to you, and with him I am sending my own heart.* ¹³*I wanted to keep him with me so that in your place he might help me while I am in prison for the Good News.* ¹⁴*But I did not want to do anything without asking you first so that any good you do for me will be because you want to do it, not because I forced you.* ¹⁵*Maybe Onesimus was separated from you for a short time so you could have him back for-ever—* ¹⁶*no longer as a slave, but better than a slave, as a loved brother. I love him very much, but you will love him even more, both as a person and as a believer in the Lord.*

¹⁷*So if you consider me your partner, welcome Onesimus as you would welcome me.* ¹⁸*If he has done anything wrong to you or if he owes you anything, charge that to me.* ¹⁹*I, Paul, am writing this with my own hand. I will pay it back, and I will say nothing about what you owe me for your own life.* ²⁰*So, my brother, I ask that you do this for me in the Lord: Refresh my heart in Christ.* ²¹*I write this letter, knowing that you will do what I ask you and even more.*

NKJV

⁸Therefore, though I might be very bold in Christ to command you what is fitting, ⁹yet for love's sake I rather appeal to you—being such a one as Paul, the aged, and now also a prisoner of Jesus Christ— ¹⁰I appeal to you for my son Onesimus, whom I have begotten while in my chains, ¹¹who once was unprofitable to you, but now is profitable to you and to me.

¹²I am sending him back. You therefore receive him, that is, my own heart, ¹³whom I wished to keep with me, that on your behalf he might minister to me in my chains for the gospel. ¹⁴But without your consent I wanted to do nothing, that your good deed might not be by compulsion, as it were, but voluntary.

¹⁵For perhaps he departed for a while for this purpose, that you might receive him forever, ¹⁶no longer as a slave but more than a slave—a beloved brother, especially to me but how much more to you, both in the flesh and in the Lord.

¹⁷If then you count me as a partner, receive him as you would me. ¹⁸But if he has wronged you or owes anything, put that on my account. ¹⁹I, Paul, am writing with my own hand. I will repay—not to mention to you that you owe me even your own self besides. ²⁰Yes, brother, let me have joy from you in the Lord; refresh my heart in the Lord.

²¹Having confidence in your obedience, I write to you, knowing that you will do even more than I say.

EXPLORATION

1. When, if ever, is it appropriate for a Christian leader, like Paul, to "pull rank" on another Christian?

2. Onesimus was a common thief who eventually became Paul's "own heart" (v. 12 NCV). How do we account for such a change?

3. What lessons on respect do you see in this postcard of an epistle?

4. Why do you think Paul didn't come right out and condemn slavery?

5. Some might argue that the situation between Onesimus and Philemon was none of Paul's business. Paul obviously felt otherwise. What are the implications of this for us?

INSPIRATION

The merciful, says Jesus, are shown mercy. They witness grace. They are blessed because they are testimonies to a greater goodness. Forgiving others allows us to see how God has forgiven us. The dynamic of giving grace is the key to understanding grace, for it is when we forgive others that we begin to feel what God feels.

Jesus told the story of a king who decided to close out all his accounts with those who worked for him (Matt. 18:21–35). He called in his debtors and told them to pay. One man owed an amount too great to return—a debt that could never be repaid. But when the king saw the man and heard his story, his heart went out to him, and he erased the debt.

As the man was leaving the palace grounds, he encountered a fellow employee who owed him a small sum. He grabbed the debtor and choked him, demanding payment. When the fellow begged for mercy, no mercy was granted. Instead, the one who had just been forgiven had his debtor thrown into jail.

When word of this got to the king, he became livid. And Jesus says, "In anger his master turned him over to the jailers to be tortured, until he should pay back all he owed" (Matt. 18:34 NIV).

Could someone actually be forgiven a debt of millions and be unable to forgive a debt of hundreds? Could a person be set free and then imprison another?

You don't have to be a theologian to answer those questions; you only have to look in the mirror. Who among us has not begged God for mercy on Sunday and then demanded justice on Monday? Who hasn't served as a bottleneck instead of a conduit of God's love? Is there anyone who doesn't, at one time or the other, *"show contempt for the riches of his [God's] kindness, tolerance and patience, not realizing that God's kindness leads you towards repentance?"* (Rom. 2:4 NIV).

Notice what God does when we calibrate our compassion. He turns us over to be tortured. Tortured by anger. Choked by bitterness. Consumed by revenge.

Such is the punishment for one who tastes God's grace but refuses to share it.

But for the one who tastes God's grace and then gives it to others, the reward is a blessed liberation. The prison door is thrown open, and the prisoner set free is yourself. (From *The Applause of Heaven* by Max Lucado)

REACTION

6. When have you been most amazed and moved by God's mercy?

7. What are the risks of seeking forgiveness? Of not seeking it?

8. What are the dangers of forgiving one who has betrayed you?

9. At some point Paul obviously suggested that Onesimus go back to his master. What do you think was said?

10. When does anger become unforgiveness and when does unforgiveness become bitterness?

11. In what relationship might God be leading you to serve as a peacemaker this week?

LIFE LESSONS

What do you do when someone slights you, rebuffs you, or intentionally hurts you? You always have a choice, you know. You can relive that affront over and over, slowly building a wall of resentment and bitterness around your heart. Regrettably, lots of people do that. Or you can, by God's grace and in his strength, elect to show supernatural mercy. Despite our wounds, and irrespective of our feelings, we *can* make the choice to forgive. What exactly is forgiveness? It is canceling the moral and personal debt another person now owes us because of his or her failure to treat us with love and respect. When we forgive, we give our offenders and the world a peek at God's heart. And we ensure that our own hearts don't become hardened.

DEVOTION

Father, forgive me for holding a grudge against _____. In the same way you have forgiven me, I want to forgive _____. Help me to learn the beautiful and rare skill of showing mercy. Remind me daily of the promise, "Blessed are the merciful, for they will be shown mercy."

For more Bible passages on forgiveness, see Micah 6:8; Matthew 5:7; Mark 11:25; Luke 6:36; 17:3–4; Ephesians 4:32; Colossians 3:13; and James 2:13.

To complete the books of Colossians and Philemon during this twelve-part study, read Philemon 1:1–25.

JOURNALING

Do we have to wait until an offender seeks forgiveness before we choose to forgive?

Lucado Life Lesson Series

Revised and updated, the Lucado Life Lessons series is perfect for small group or individual use and includes intriguing questions that will take you deeper into God's Word.

THOMAS NELSON
Since 1798

Available at your local Christian Bookstore.